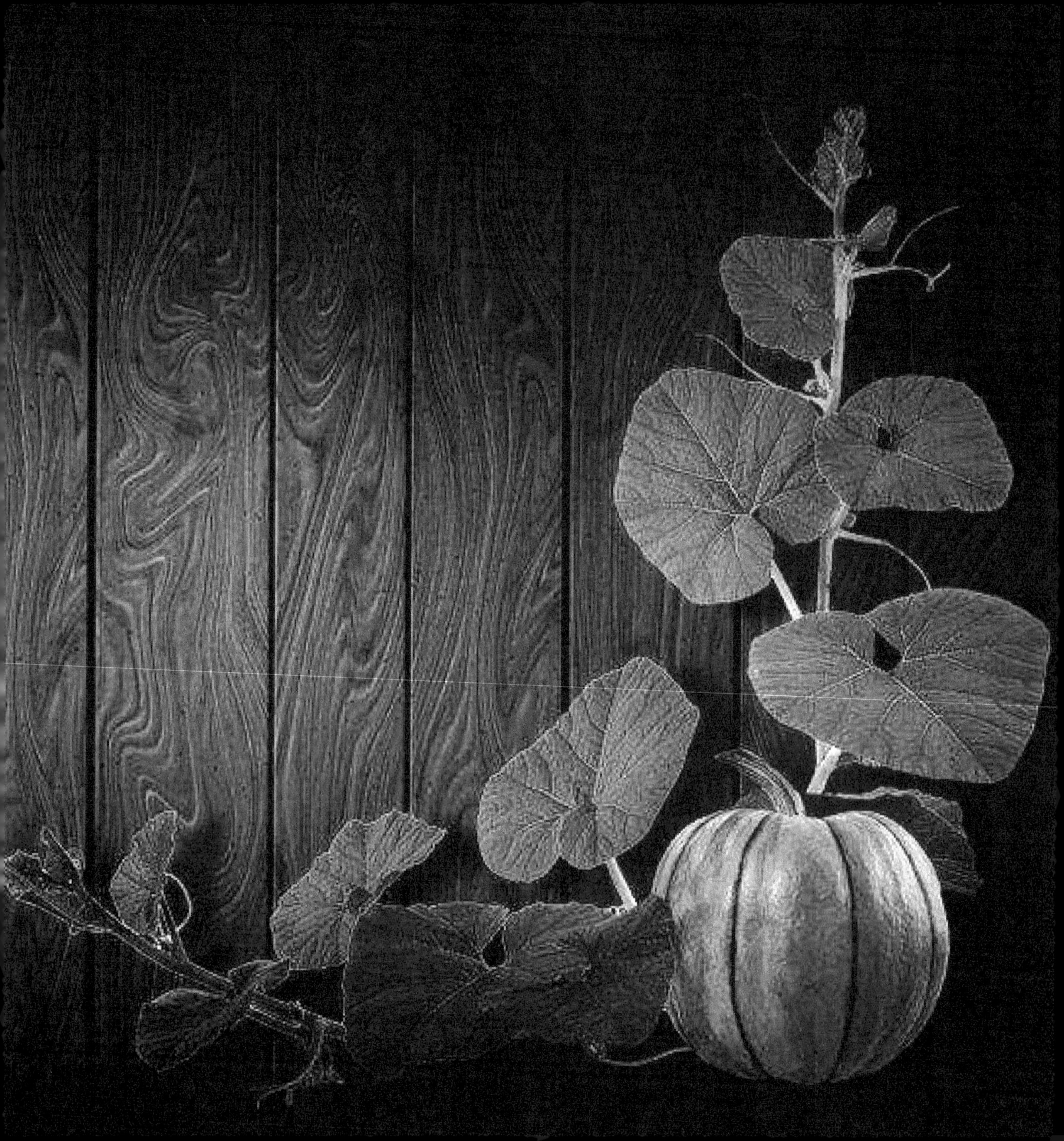

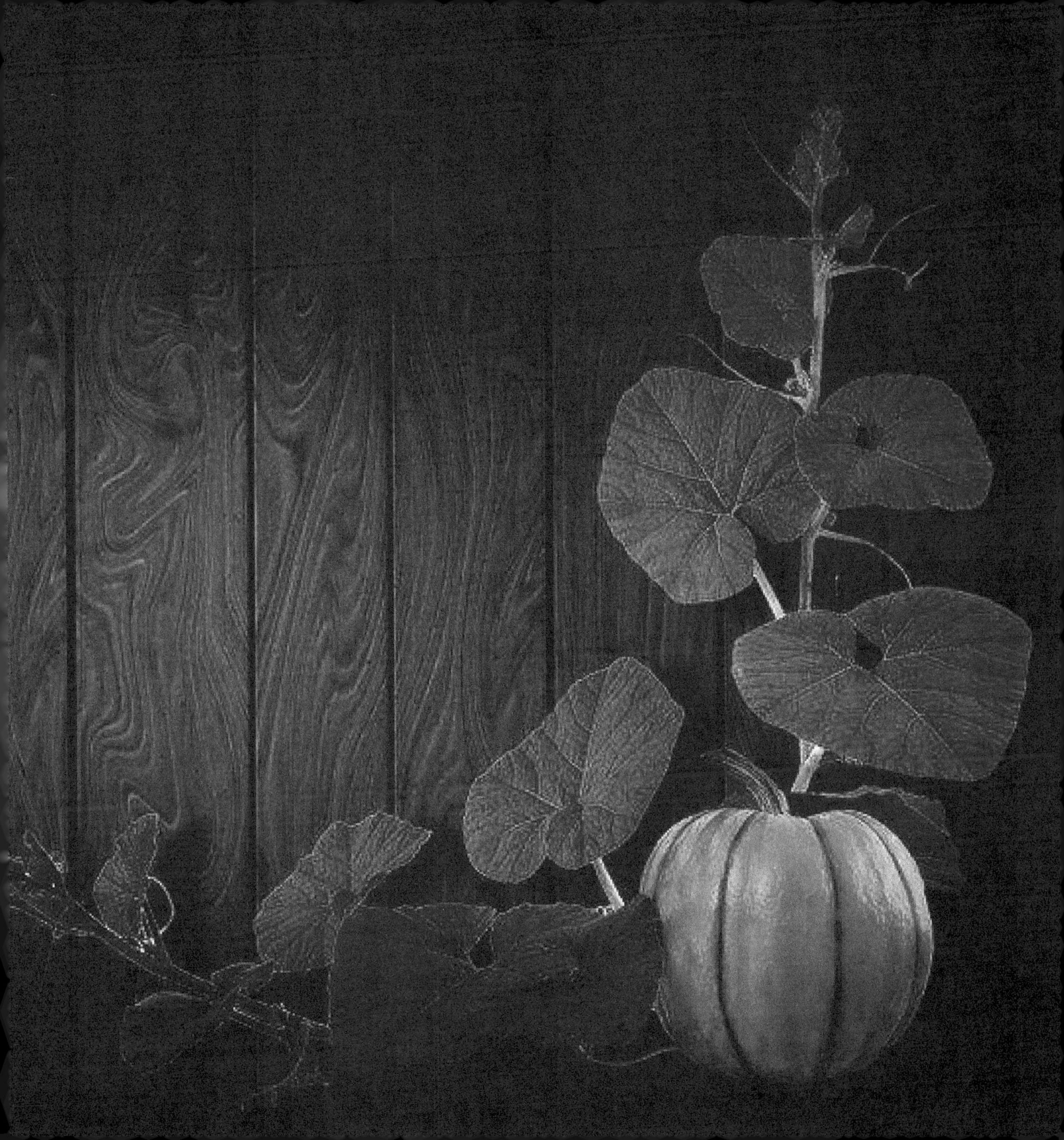

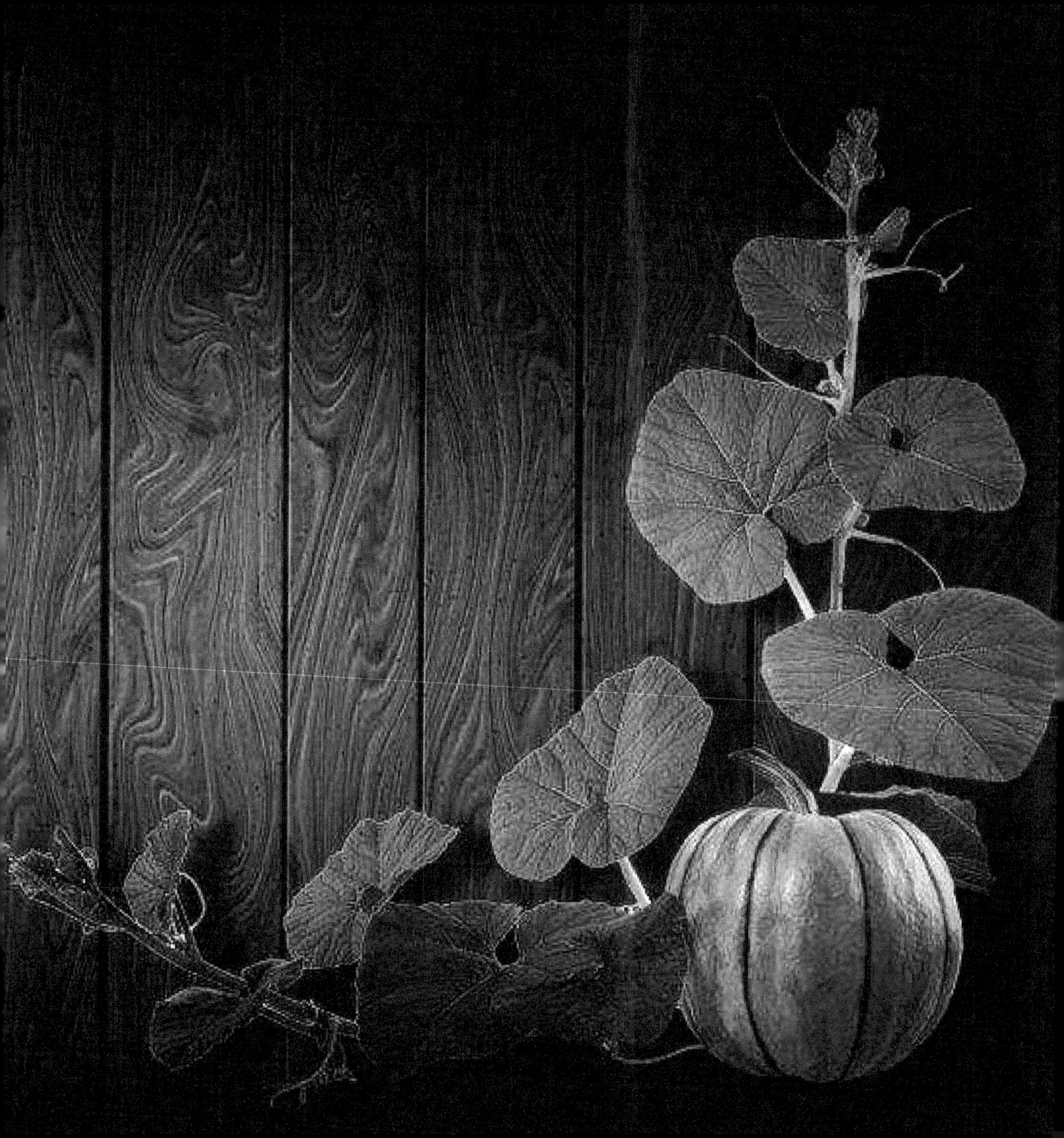

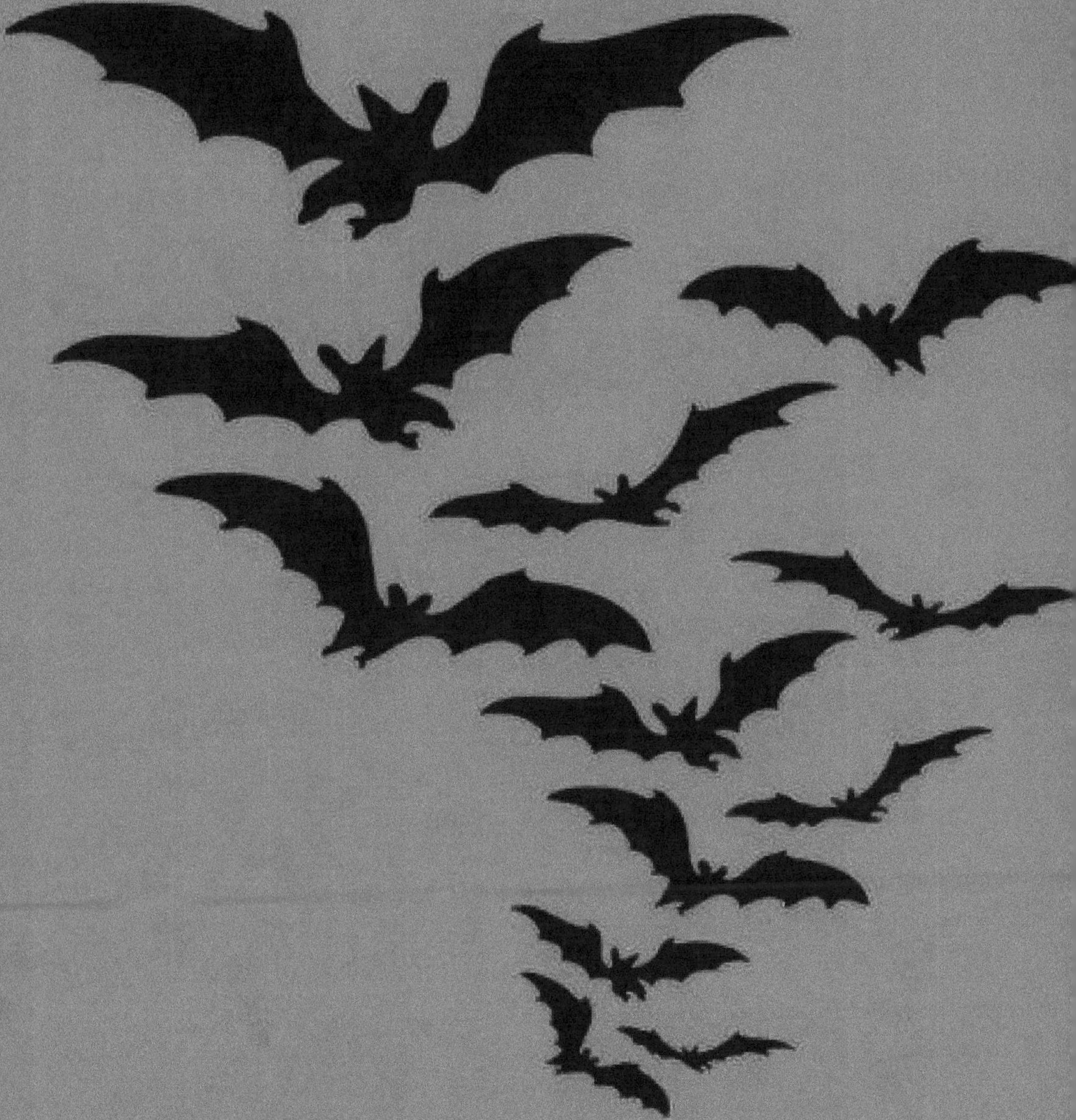

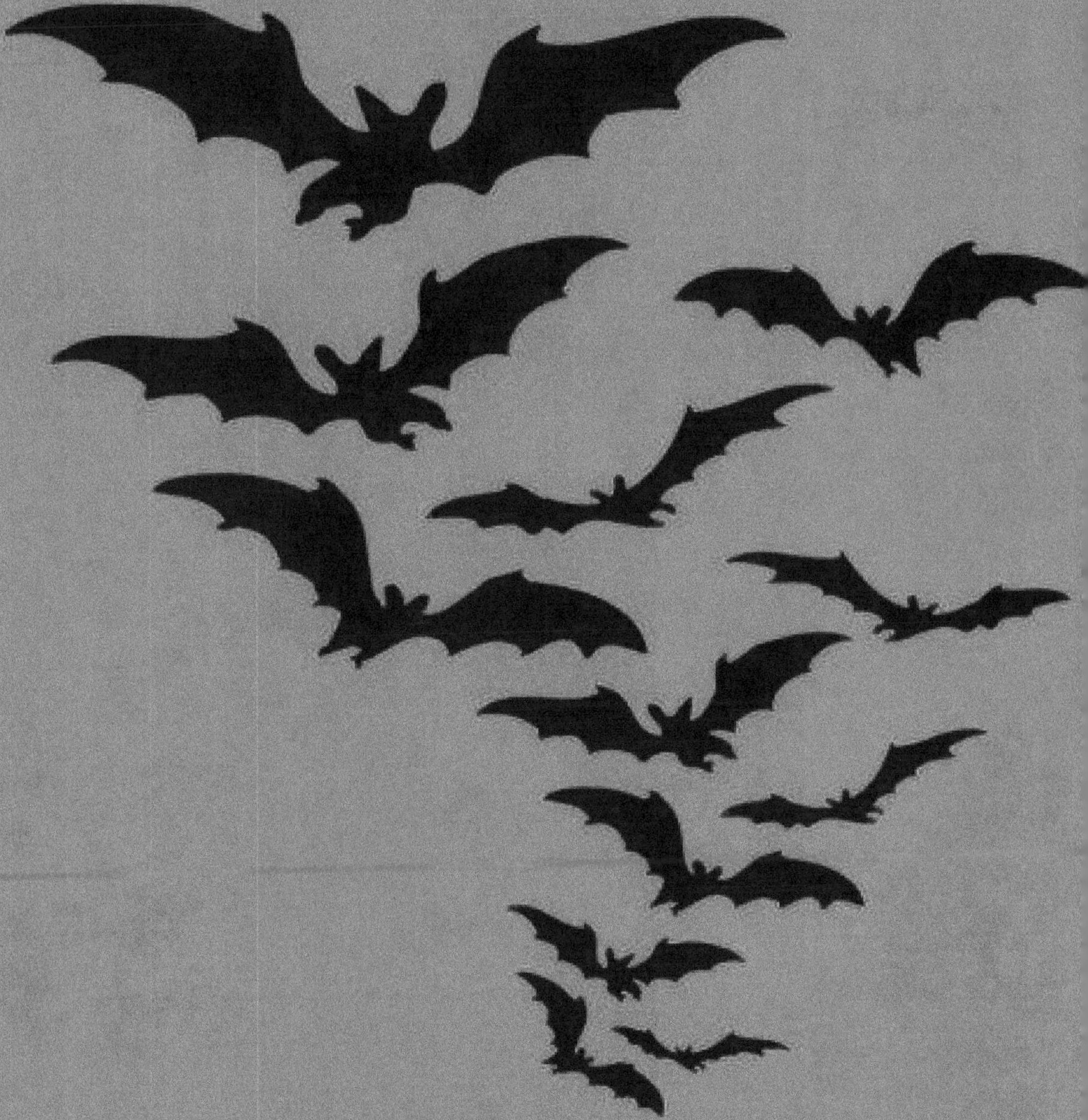

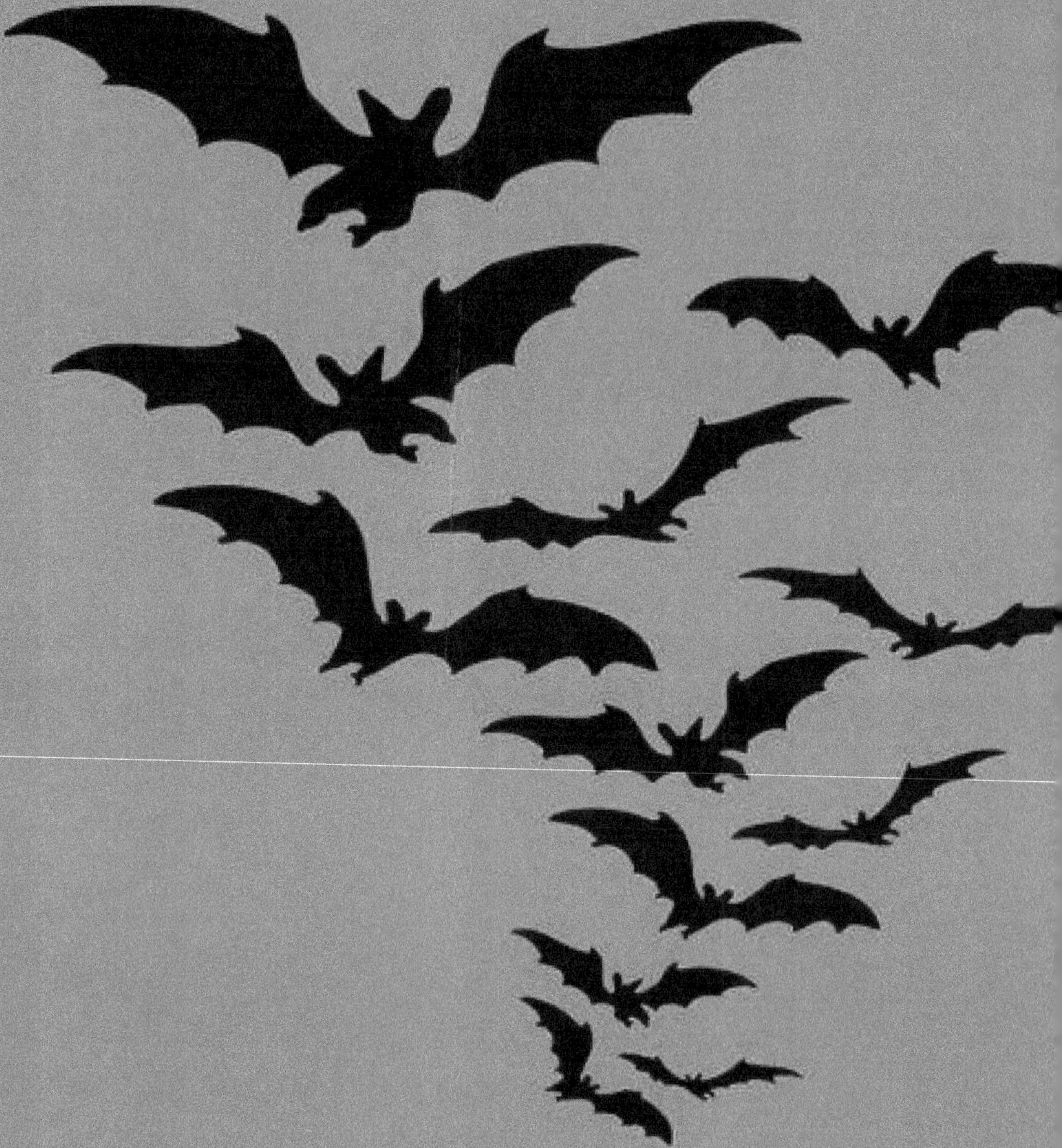

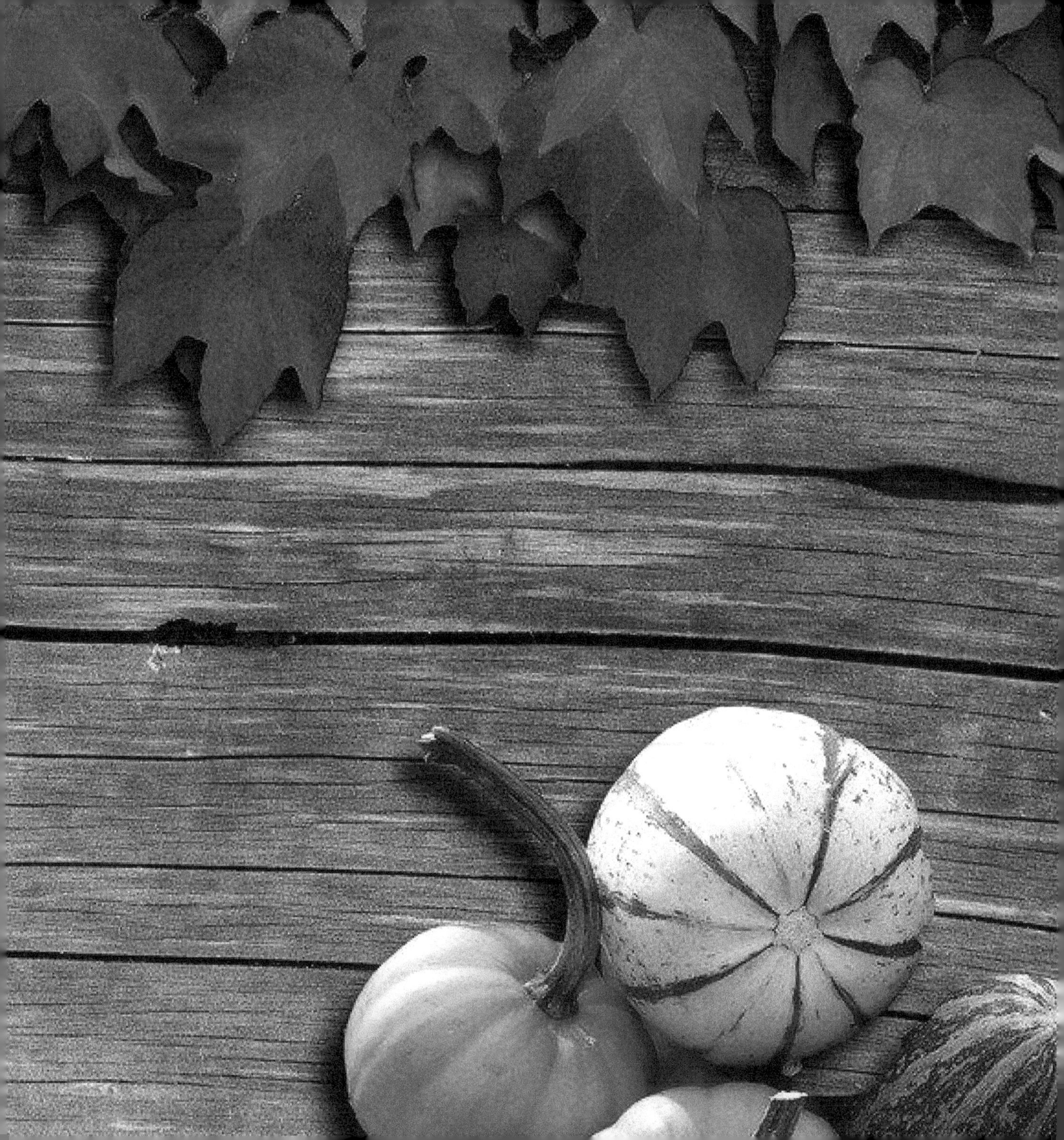

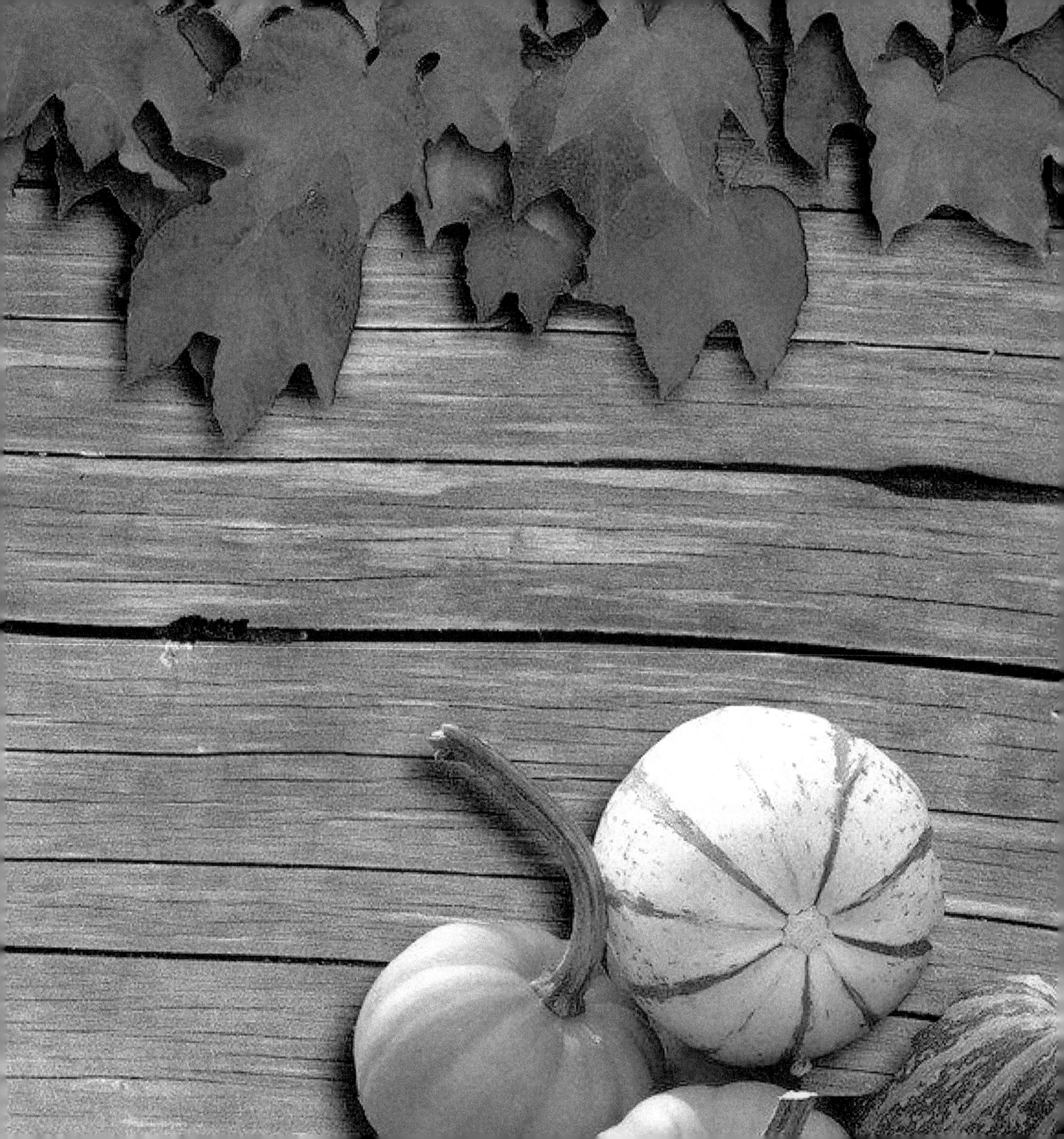

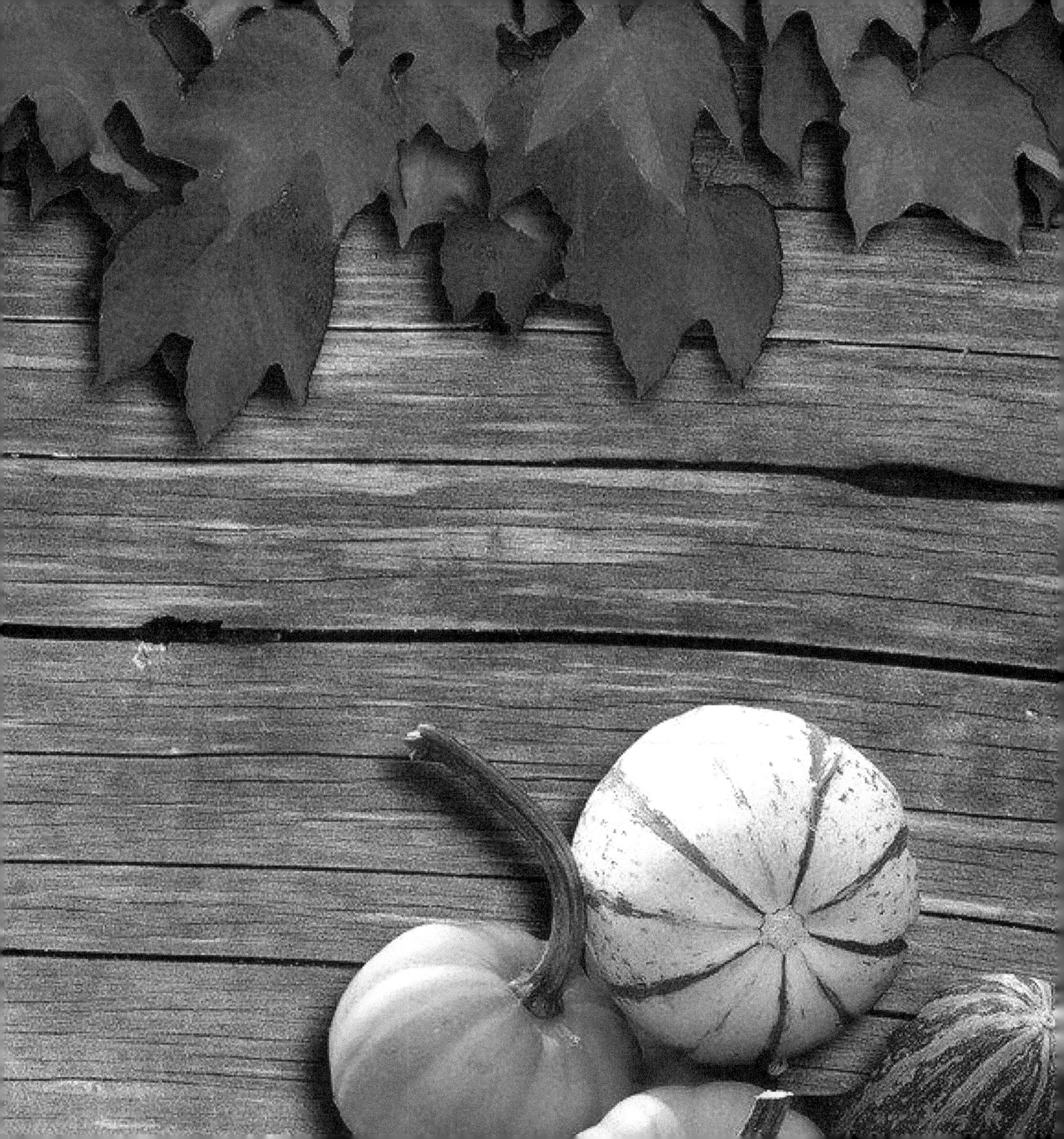

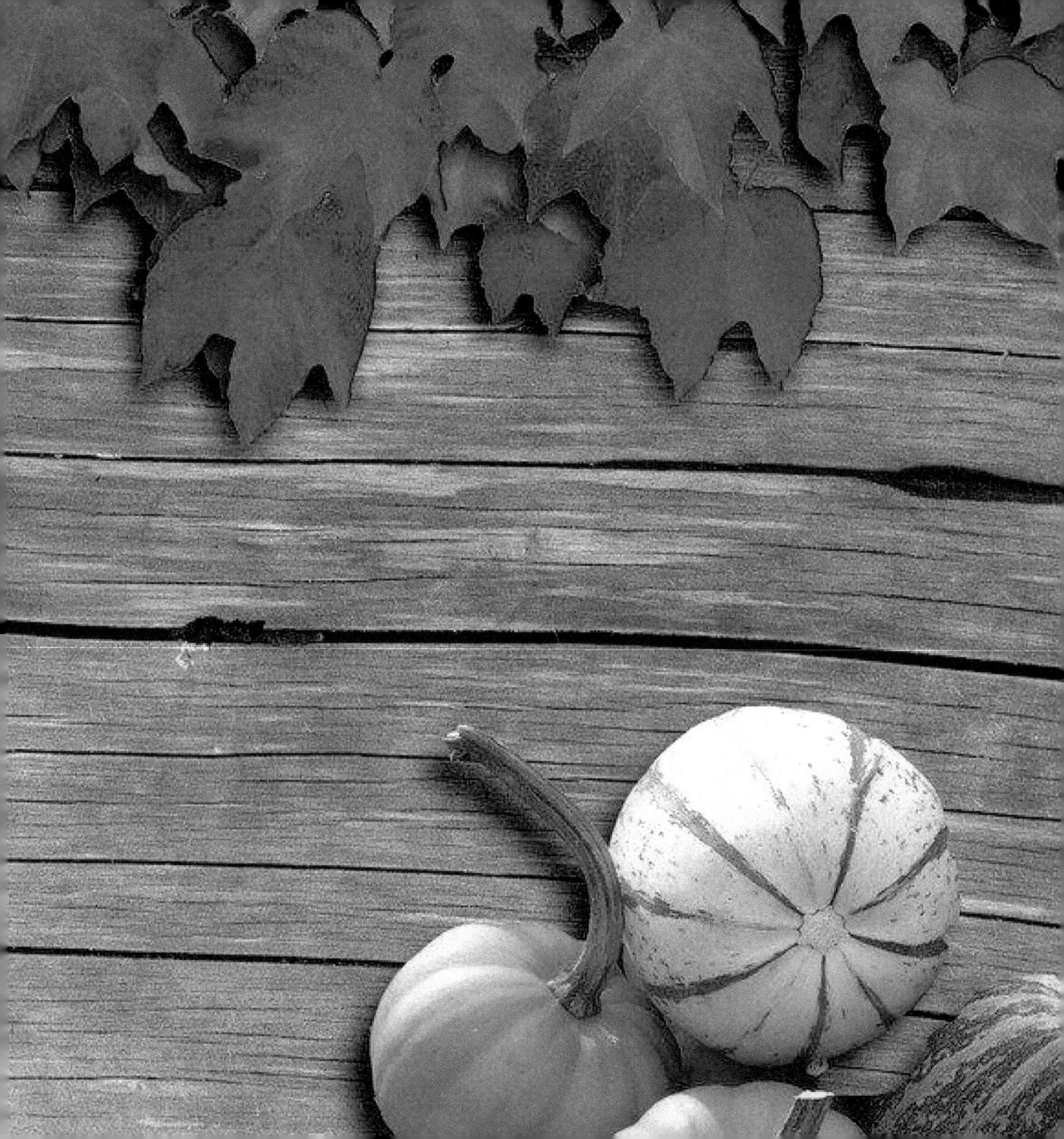

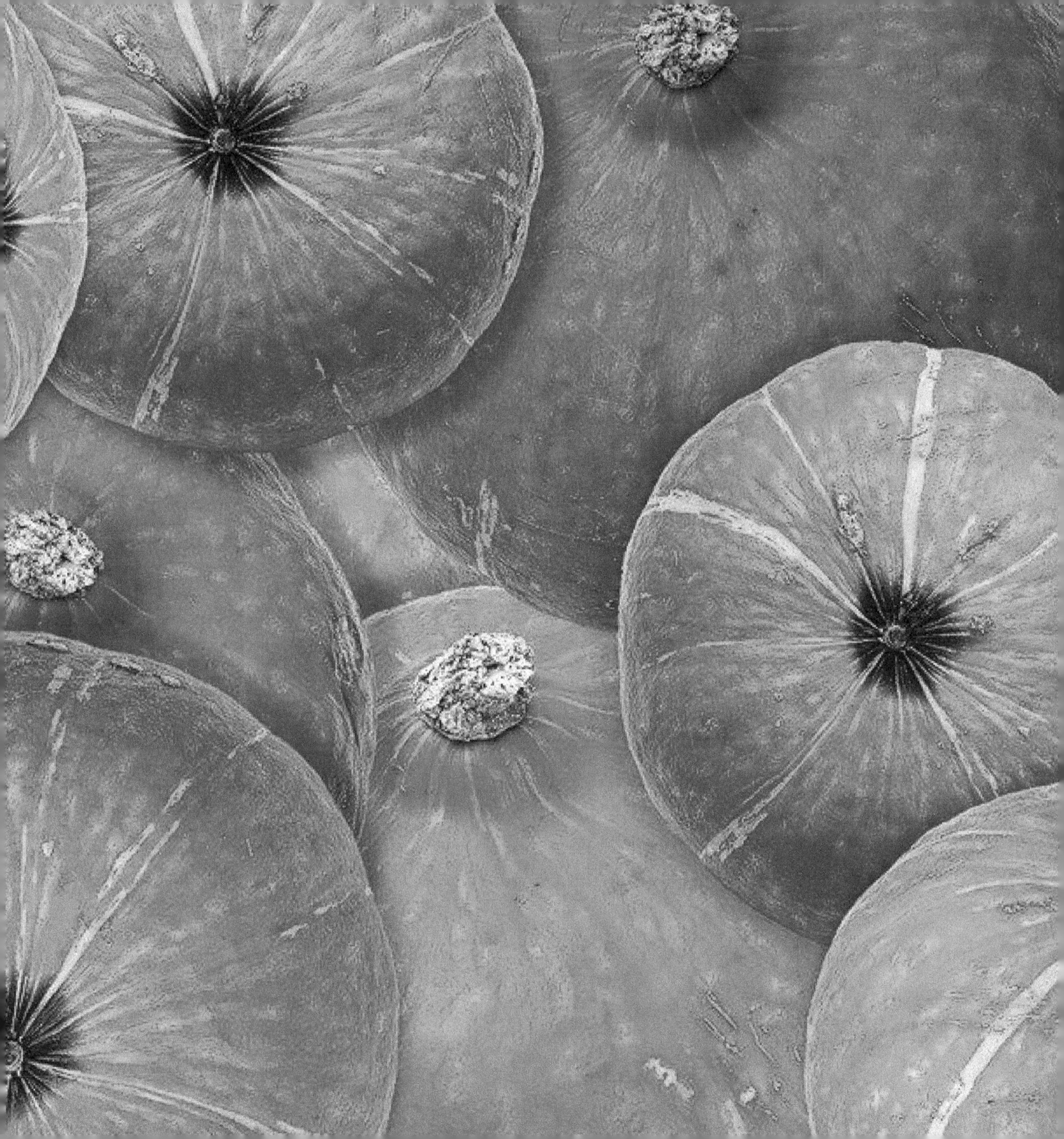

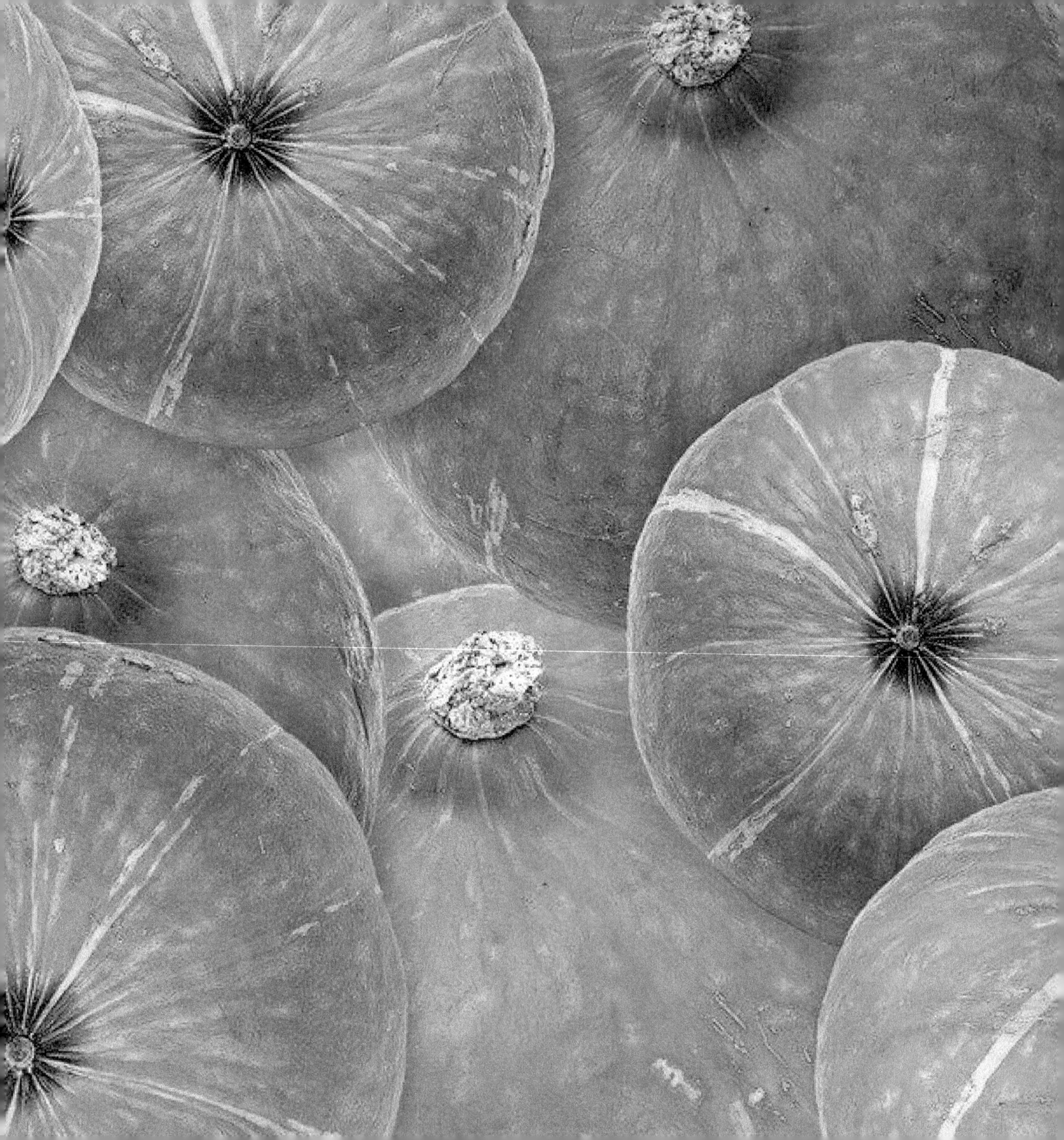

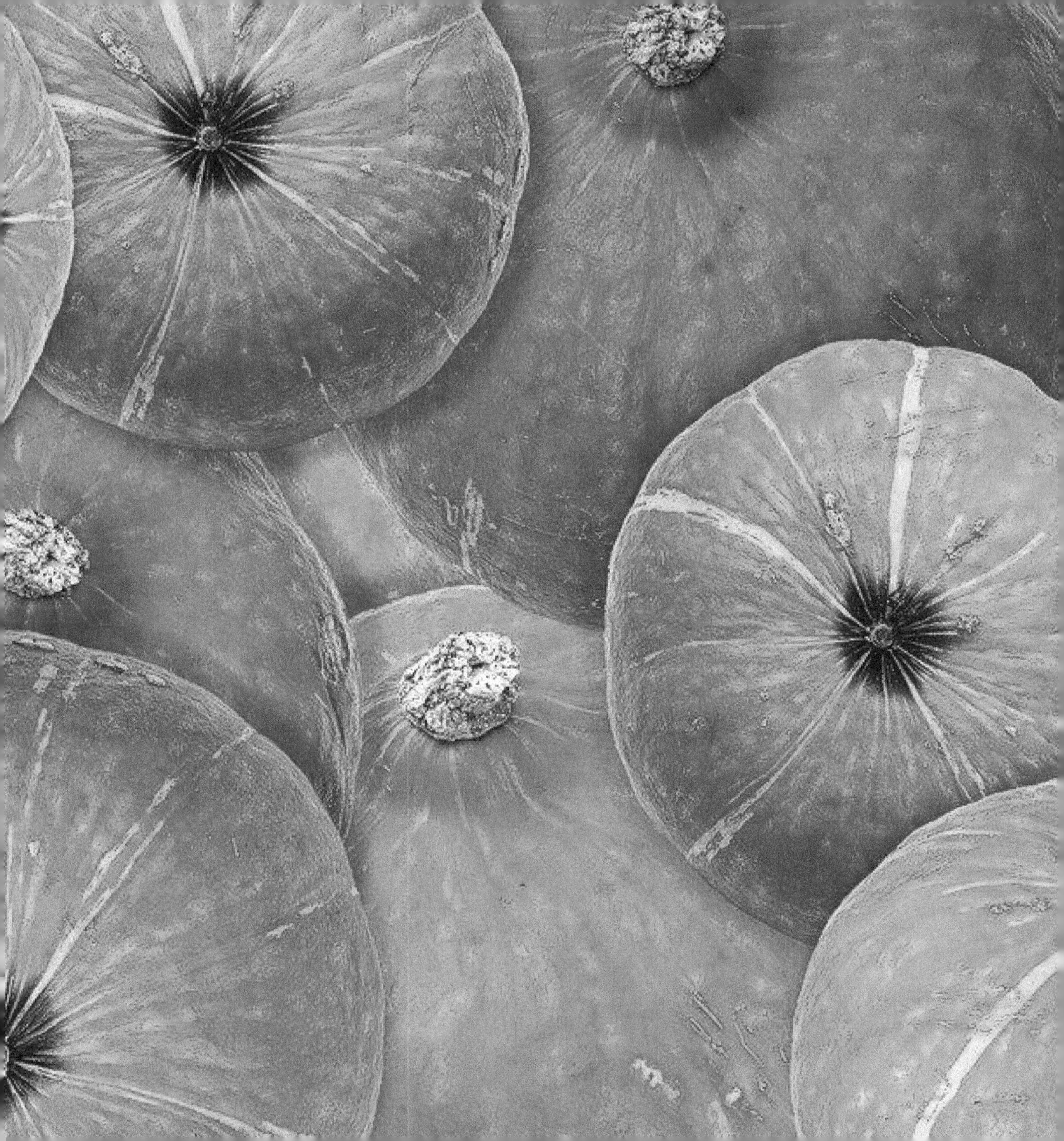

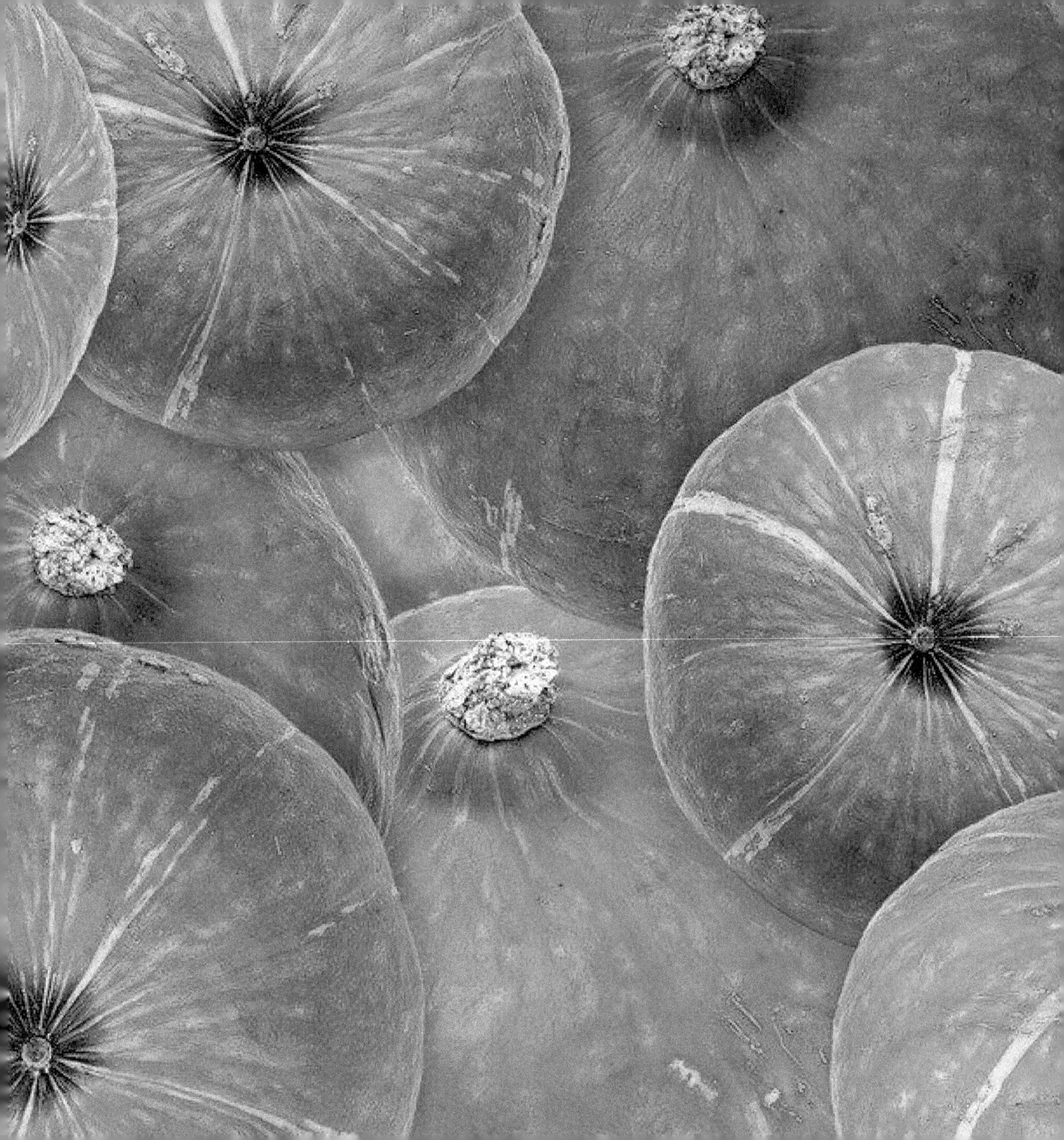

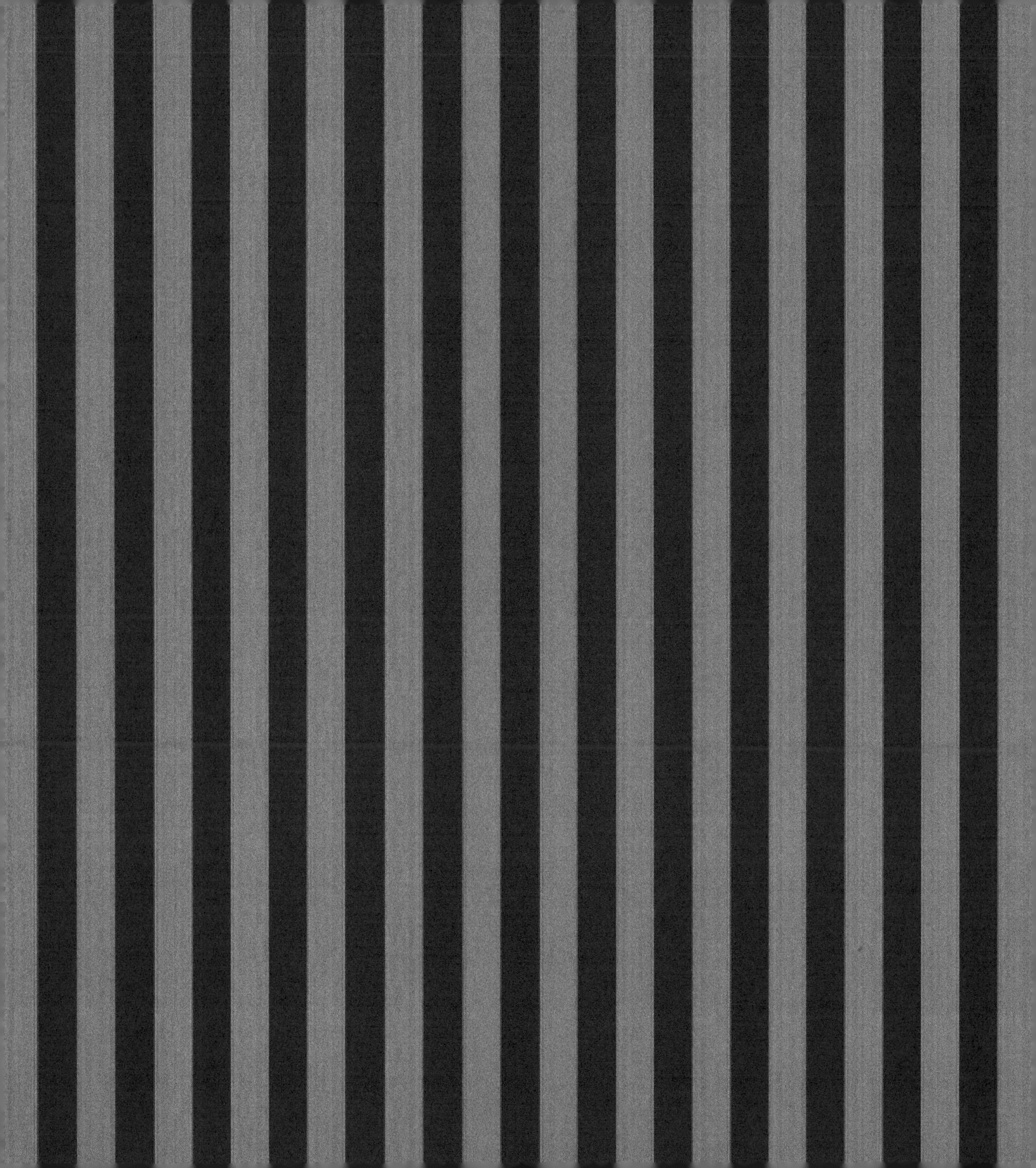

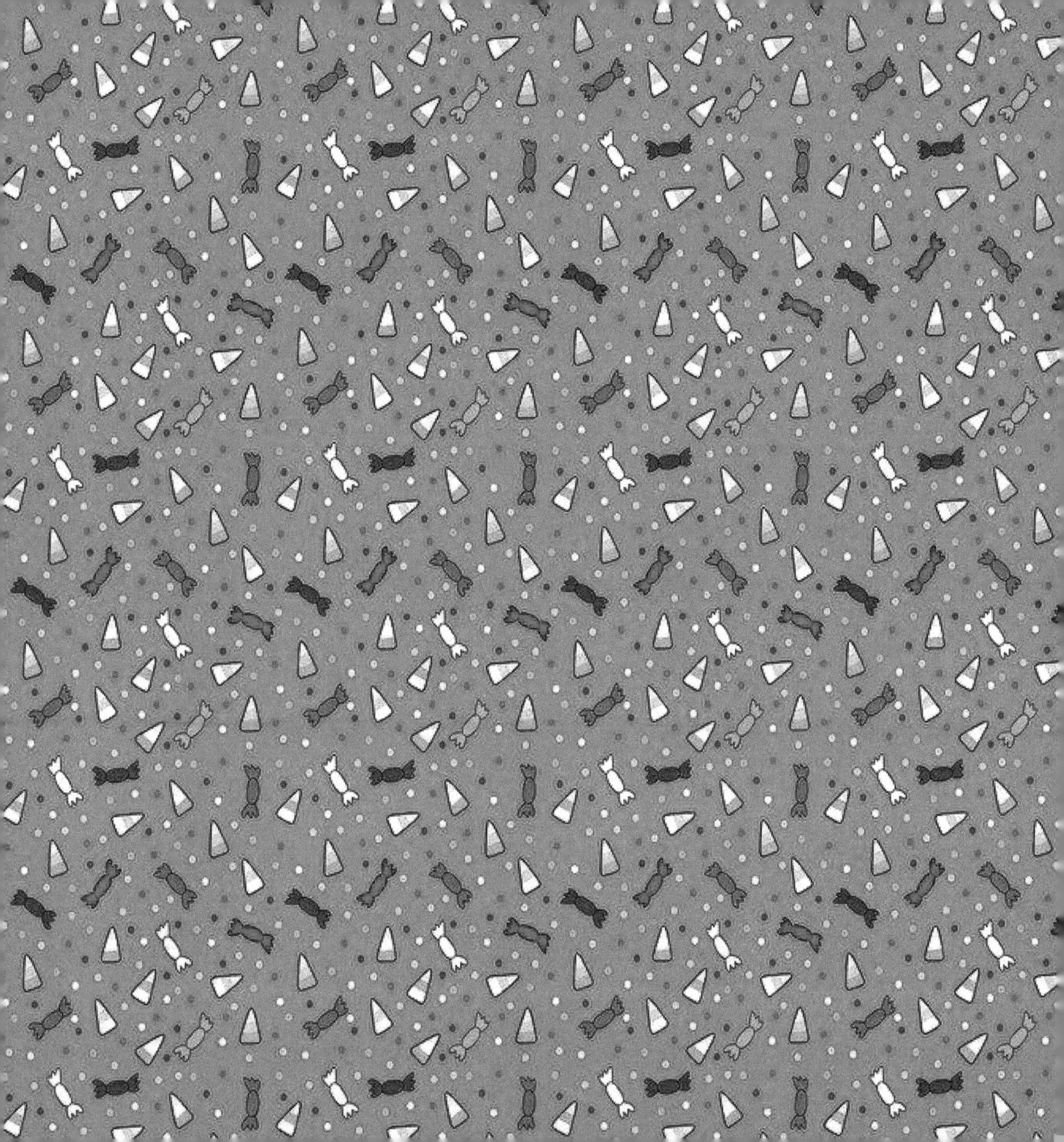

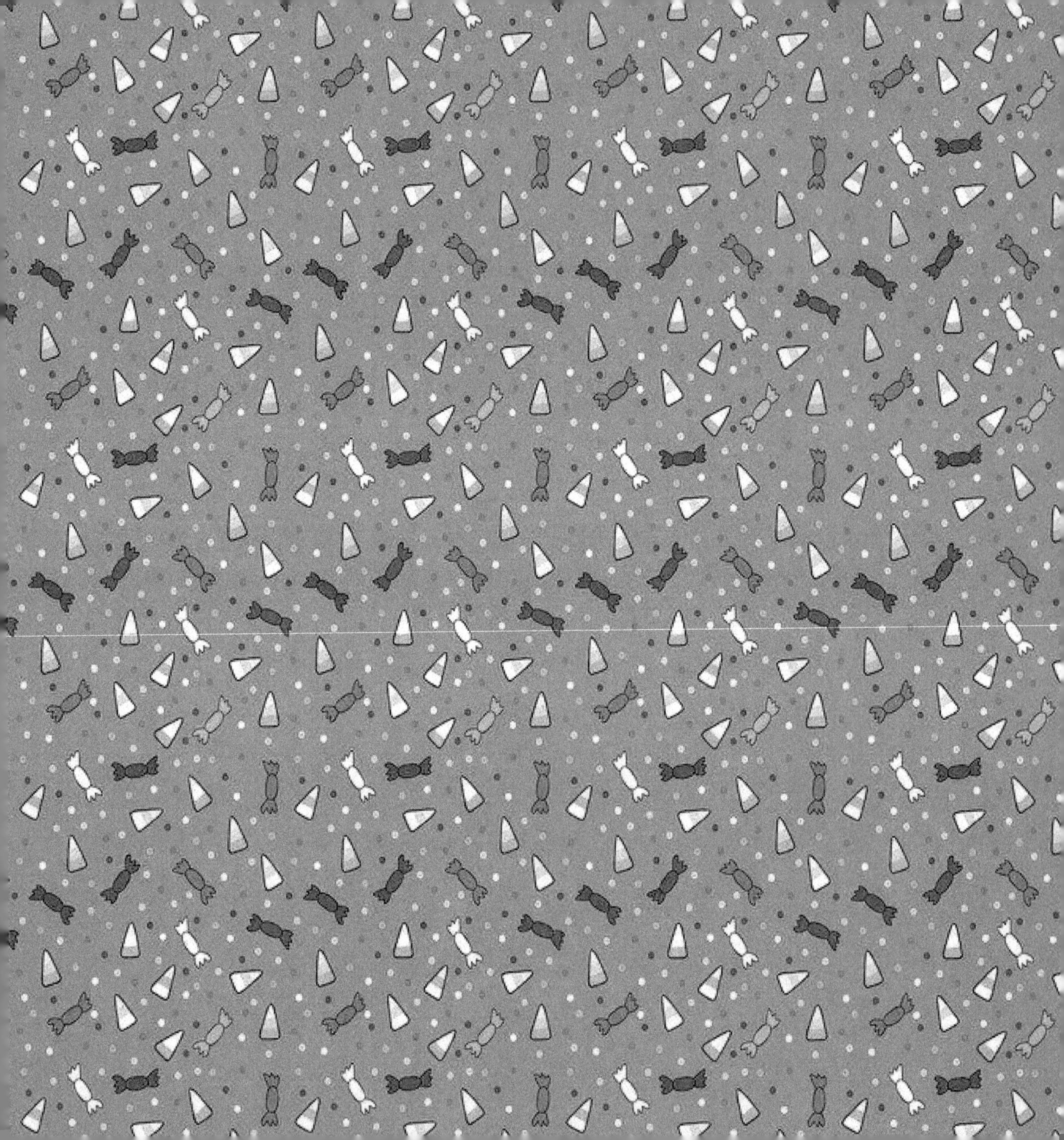

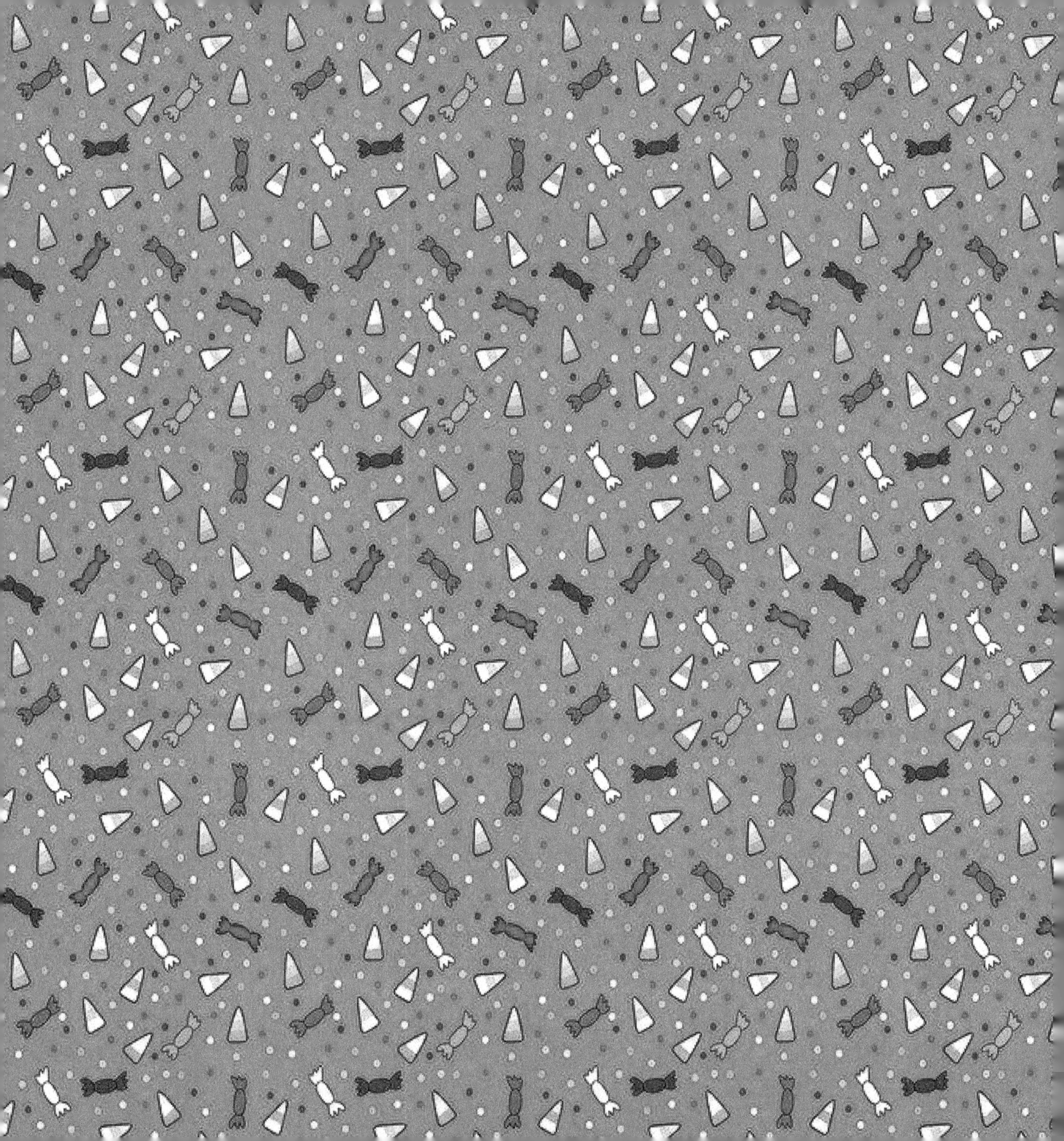

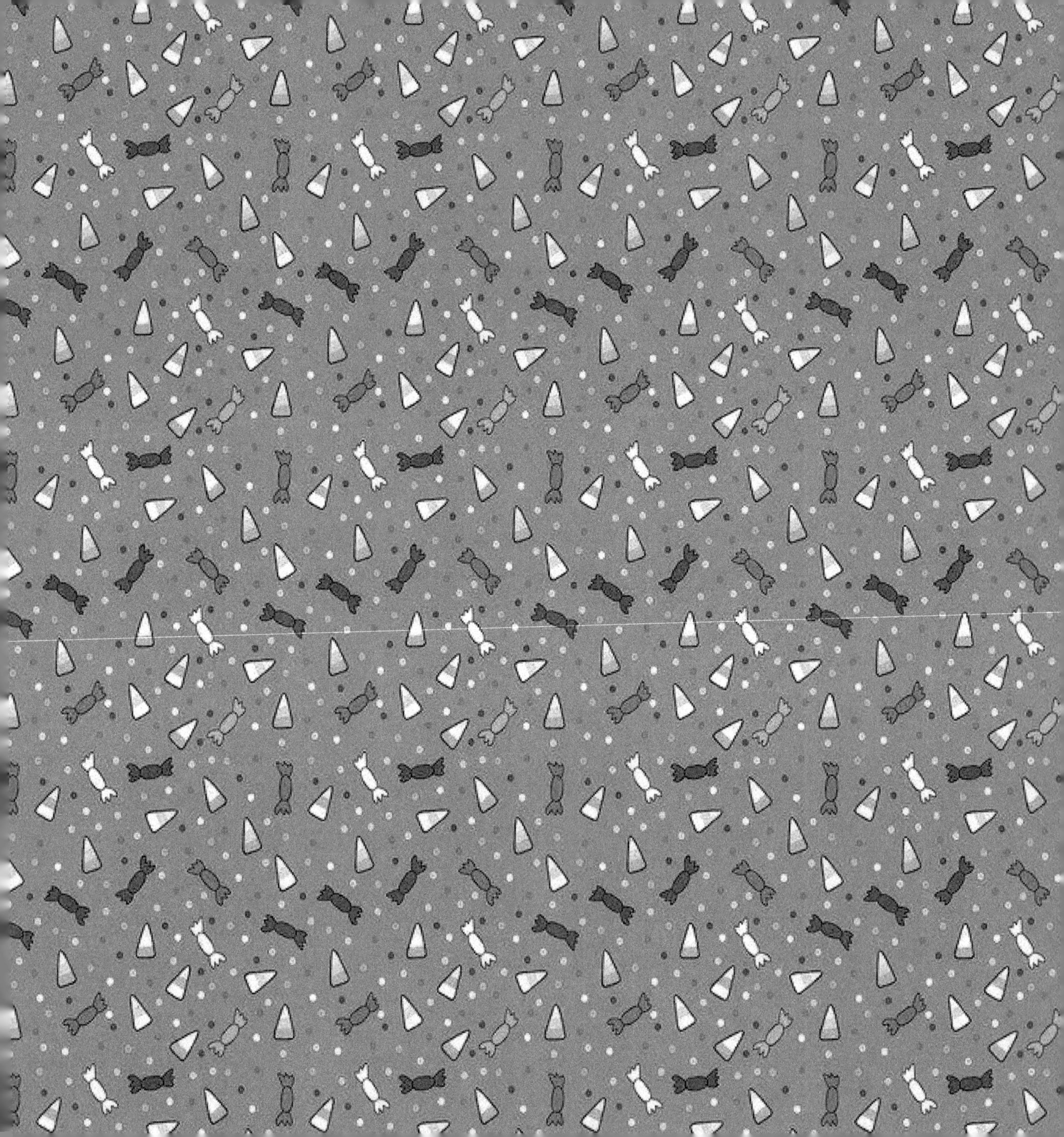

Printed in the USA
CPSIA information can be obtained
at www.ICGtesting.com
LVHW080738271023
762071LV00013B/477

9 781951 373535